# Profit Power

## Ten Strategies to

## Blueprint a Dynamic

## Construction Business

*By Paul Montelongo*

**"America's Construction
Industry Motivator"**

Published by Success Concepts Inc.

Success Concepts Inc.
1141 N. Loop 1604 East
Suite 105, PMB 407
San Antonio, Texas 78232
Toll Free: 866.494.1911
Email: Paul@ContractorOfChoice.com
Website: www.ContractorOfChoice.com

ISBN 1-59196-437-7

# Dedication

This book is dedicated to all of the women and men in the construction business who have attended my seminars, workshops, and speeches, or read my books, articles, and newsletters over the past four years. Thank you for continuing to challenge me to find answers to your concerns about your business.

To you, the professional contractor who goes out into your community everyday to hustle and build high quality projects that bears your name and seal of approval. It isn't always easy or risk free. But somehow, when the sawdust settles, it sure is rewarding.

# Contents

# Contents

# INTRODUCTION

Let's get this project started.

As with any new project that you are about to start, there is a measure of excitement and anticipation. It doesn't matter how long you have been in the construction business. Once you have spent weeks or months preparing a bid and you are awarded the project, there is an expectation of profits and project success.

This is a unique book. It is a compilation of material that I have been working on for a couple of years. I have literally written tens of thousands of words for articles, newsletters, speeches, seminar curriculum, website copy and other sources. As I travel and speak to construction organizations and associations around the country, I have interviewed hundreds of contractors just like you. I always ask what is working and what needs to be improved in the industry.

The book that you are about to read is a collection of the best of the best. From my articles, newsletters, and the aforementioned writings, I have accumulated the top ten strategies that the most successful contractors in the country use to help them increase their profit power. I have expanded the scope of these strategies to explain why they work and how they will benefit you.

The concepts are simple and direct, and the best part is that you can do the strategies immediately. There are two chapters on sales. Fierce competition in the industry seems to be affecting sales more than ever.

There is a chapter dedicated to getting top dollar for your product and service. There is a chapter relating to a unique way to have more satisfactory customer relationships. There is a chapter to help you win more bids and then, there is my favorite chapter of all. It is chapter seven, which discusses publicity and promotion.

**Chapter four is the most profound in the book**. It takes a total "out of the tool box" look at what it takes to be successful in this business. My suggestion is that you read it and regularly meditate on the points made in the chapter.

The remaining chapters include the topic of leadership, creating systems and building a dynamic team of motivated people. Each chapter has specific steps and strategies that you can immediately implement.

This is not a long, drawn out book. As contractors, you have told me that you like to get to the point. You want to know what to do and you want it in a hurry. I believe you and I wrote this book to that end.

I should know. For more than twenty-six years I have been working along side you as a design/build remodeling contractor, homebuilder and insurance renovation specialist in the highly competitive south Texas market.

About four years ago, in 1999, I was asked to deliver a speech to a group of contractors. I taught selling skills, goal setting and marketing strategies. The things I taught had helped me build a successful business and raise a fine family. The program was a success and as destiny would have it, that was certainly not the last seminar I would deliver. Now, I am a full time professional trainer and business strategist to the construction industry. In this capacity, I have trained thousands of contractors just like you. I continue to ask a few simple questions. What is working in your business? What are your greatest successes? What keeps you up at night staring at the ceiling about your business? I will keep searching for the answers to these questions and reporting my findings to you.

My mission now in the industry is to continue to raise the level of professionalism. I want mainstream America to view contractors as a viable, professional, profit-deserving enterprise. I am on a personal mission to dispel the notion that most contractors are "Bubbas" working out of the back of their truck.

Once you read this book and implement the concepts, you will be helping to elevate the professional level of our industry. Together, let's send a message to the modern consumer that contractors are genuinely interested in building dynamic businesses that create jobs, expand the economy and give people a first class place to live, recreate, worship and raise decent families.

Oh, by the way, Profit Power will help you increase your bottom line and build a dynamic construction business.

Until we meet in person, take great care of yourself and your loved ones.

*Paul Montelongo*

# CHAPTER ONE:

## BE A SALES MAGNET

### *5 ways to be instantly irresistible*

I recently saw a poster in a sporting goods store of the three stooges. Larry, Curly and Moe were slovenly dressed, holding their golf clubs and looking comfortably smug in each other's presence. The title of the poster was ... "Play Golf with Your Friends." After a good chuckle, I was reminded of the truth in this statement. People tend to choose their friends and associates because of the perception of similarities with them.

Successful construction entrepreneurs understand the longevity of their enterprise depends on the relationship and bond that is built with clients, vendors and prospective customers. How do you make more sales, open more quality alliances, and have better customer relationships in the highly competitive construction business? Rapport is the key.

Your ability to create an unbreakable bond and to establish trust and confidence is crucial. Everyone has a reality. In other words, what is real to you is very personal. What is real to me is equally personal. Everyone tends to believe that their way of communicating is the right way, at least for him or her. In order to magnetize people to you and your service, you must enter their reality. You must assume their reality.

Here are the five most effective ways to create instant and lasting rapport with anyone you meet.

1.  **Express a genuine interest in the other person and in what is important to them.**

The operative word here is *genuine.* Get very curious about the other person and satisfy your curiosity by asking personal questions. Ask leading questions to elicit details about their family, hobbies, career, and business. Do this in an effort to find things in common. Your customer will enjoy this kind of conversation because it will be a different experience for them. Most contractors just want to get down to the business of building something. A personal conversation with your customer puts you on a different plane with them. It makes you unique and most people love to visit with unique individuals.

Use their personal name often. The sweetest sound to people is the sound of their own name. Make mental or written notes of the important events and activities in their life. Refer to these as often as possible. It is amazing how people love to talk about themselves. When you have a genuine interest in your customer, they will open up and really tell you what they want in the business relationship. They will also be more apt to listen to what you want.

## 2. Create physical rapport.

Since you tend to relate more easily to those who are like you in some way, establishing physical rapport is a skill to develop. This is sometimes called matching, mirroring, or parroting. Try to match the body language, vocabulary and tone of voice of the other person.

For example, your customer may use animated gestures. They may speak slowly and softly. This is their reality. In order not to offend them, you must be a reflection of their communication style. This allows you to more readily understand and empathize with the person's position. Why? Because, though you may be different, you are similar in many aspects. Most humans tend to have the same body language for similar emotions. If you adjust your body language slightly to match the other person, you begin to find likeness with the other person. This shows respect and adds validity to what the person is saying while allowing you to experience some of the same reactions.

## 3. Be an active listener.

The best communicators in the world have the ability to listen at least four times more than they speak. Listening attentively enables you to discern what the real issues are by what is said and, in many cases, by what is not said. Paraphrasing what has been said or asking re-direct questions validate that the other person has been heard. It usually leads to more clarity about what is really being said.

Again, people love to talk more than they like to listen. The listener controls the conversation. Active listening helps you discern how the other person processes information. Is your customer looking for visual aids? Will they learn more if you verbally describe your service or must they be motivated by the sense or feeling of what you have to offer? When these processing styles are determined, you then can present your case in a way that they will most likely appreciate.

Two key components of active listening are verification and validation. To verify that you have heard your customer the way that you think you have heard them, simply ask, "Do I understand you to mean ...?" Or, you may say something like, "By that, do you mean ...?"

To validate your customer's conversation, you must accentuate the points upon which you agree. You may say something like: "I completely agree with what you said about the size of your house." Or, you may say something like, "I totally see your point when you say that the oak trees must be protected during the construction process."

## 4.   Seek agreement.

It is easier to move from agreement to agreement than from disagreement to agreement. Search for as many ways as possible to reach similarities with your customers. The easiest area to reach agreement is with your language. Avoid nomenclature and construction jargon that is unfamiliar to your customer.

Construction industry folks tend to use similar phrases and terminology. Your customer may know some of the lingo and may be lost with other terms. Make completely sure that your customer knows what you are talking about at all times.

Look for beliefs or opinions that you share in common. This is different from adopting another person's beliefs. Rather, acknowledge the fundamental commonalties that may be woven in the other person's opinion. On rare occasions, you may have to agree to disagree.

Though rare, this is a form of agreement and it may build enough respect for opening an ongoing relationship. Seeking agreement requires flexibility. It means that you may need to adjust your perception of the situation in order to move to agreement. Agreement of even the minutest details provides a foundation for broader agreement.

## 5. Be genuinely friendly.

There is absolutely no substitute for being friendly. I mean being real. A smile and an agreeable disposition usually will diffuse any tense situation long before it happens. When it is real, it builds long-term trust and credibility.

You certainly know when someone is not being sincere with you about his or her product or service. Give your customer the same courtesy. After all, don't you like to deal with people who are pleasant? That doesn't mean you have to be the bubbly cheerleader type. A sincere smile, a warm handshake and good manners go a long way. Their impact is subtle and often remains long after you leave.

Having a friendly, gentle, sincere disposition is frequently overlooked in the construction industry. Since that is the case, it is even more impressive when it is a part of your personal protocol.

To build profit power in your construction business, these strategies will greatly enhance your ability to create strong bonds and lasting relationships. Here is a secret. They are also a fantastic way to build better family and personal relationships. Selling your product or services in this day and age is about **OPENING** relationships rather than just *closing* deals. It is estimated that 80% of the time, you purchase the products you do based on how you feel about the person who is selling them to you. In service-related industries, like construction, the percentage is even higher. In other words, do you like the person that is selling to you? Is he or she trustworthy? Do his or her business and personal interests resemble yours? These are questions that most buyers ask themselves at a conscious or a sub-conscious level. Simply stated, you buy much more often from those people you like.

# CHAPTER TWO:

# GET TOP DOLLAR

## *Establish value to get what you are worth*

Do you get **Top Dollar** for every project you perform?  Or, like many contractors, do you give a little here and there to make the price work for your client in hopes that you will turn enough profit to make the project worth your while?  In a fiercely competitive market place, there is little room for "padding" your bids.  When you know that you are worth every cent of your contract price, how do you get top dollar for your product or service?

The answer is to "repackage for value."  Adding greater value to your service and letting your clients know about this value is the key to getting **Top Dollar**.  By "repackaging for value," you set your company apart from the crowd to get what you really want.  Offering real value for your product or service will allow you to justify your price in the minds of your customers.

Where do you start? First, understand that most of the time, value is only a perception. Value is one of those business buzzwords that are only defined by the prospective buyer. The individual client determines value. What is of value to one client may be of little value to another. For example, an extended warranty offer may mean little to a person who is only interested in a convenient and temporary solution. What compels one customer to buy means little or nothing to another customer.

How do you know what to offer? It requires a little homework, but not much. Start with your existing client database and just ask. That's right - ask your premier customer what they consider to be the real value in what you do.

The key is that you must ask your premier customer. Your premier customer is that customer who has a high level of need for your product. They also have a frequent need for your product and they are in a position to influence others to buy your product. Your premier customer understands the value of what you do, so just ask them. You may obtain this information in a personal interview, by way of questionnaire, and certainly by observing the buying patterns of your customer.

From these interviews, discern what it is that you do that sets you apart from the competition. This is your customer's perception of the value of your product or service. When you interview enough of your customers, you will begin to hear a repeating theme. It is this theme that you want to accentuate in all of your marketing, sales and promotion efforts.

Some areas to consider that will set your product apart from the competition are as follows:

## *Responsiveness*

In a fast paced society where people expect things to be "done yesterday," response time is crucial. Response time relates to returning phone calls, on-time or before-time delivery, warranty response, real-time quotations, etc. Response time correlates to customer service. The promptness and quality of the response time often is a measure of exquisite customer service.

When interviewing your premiere customer, ask how they define responsiveness. Is it five minutes, five hours, two days or somewhere in between? Responsiveness requires listening to your customer and delivering according to their expectations. Again, your premier customer will tell you how responsive you are and what you can do to improve.

## *Knowledge*

What information do you possess that is important to your customer? Even better, what information do you possess that your competition has yet to discover? There is great value in knowing information that will enhance the purchase your customer is about to make.

It is interesting that in our society, there is a plethora of information that is available. Your customer is very savvy. Not only do they know what you know; they know what you should know. Therefore, they are interested in the application of the knowledge. The knowledge that you have obtained through education or experience is of great value to your customer. How you intend to apply your knowledge to your customer's project is what they really want to know.

When your knowledge improves your customer's personal or professional well being, your product or service has tremendous value. You may have vital information about safety, design, practicality, or time and money savings. When you demonstrate to your customer how your knowledge benefits their life, you have created enormous value.

Ask your premiere customer how the application of your knowledge benefited them. The answers you receive become valuable to your future clients and to you.

## *Quality of Product or Service*

In order to get **Top Dollar**, there must be a distinguishable difference between you and your competition. You must be able to demonstrate a higher level of quality with your product or service. When you are able to prove the higher level of quality, the marginal difference in cost is justifiable. Your customer can then amortize the cost difference over the life of the product and the real value will shine through.

How do you prove that you deliver higher quality than your competition? Among many things, the quality of your product can be measured by durability, life expectancy, ease of use or maintenance standards. Maintain copious records of your customers' feedback.

Have you implemented a system that has reduced warranty calls? Are you able to speed up the delivery time on your projects? Do you have a special strategy for helping your customer make design selections? Tracking the results of these techniques and reporting the results to your prospective customers can distinguish your company above the competition. The point is that there are many ways to improve the quality of your product or service to add real value for your customer.

## *Variables*

You would probably be surprised at the many responses customers give when asked why they buy a specific product from a company. In addition to the aforementioned reasons, there are many intangible reasons that your customer will consider as value.

Your premier customer may say that you and your company staff are easy to work with. Perhaps you have made the purchasing process easy for them. They may buy from you based solely on your reputation. They may just like the color and design of your brochure. Perhaps you have longevity in your marketplace.

There can be any number of reasons why a customer will buy your product. Continue to ask your best customers why they buy from you. What forms the basis of their buying decisions? Keep track of these reasons and emphasize them to prospective customers. Odds are that they too have some of the same needs as your existing customers.

It is not easy to command **Top Dollar** in an intensely competitive marketplace unless you understand how to "repackage for value". Take great care in asking your premier customers what makes your company stand apart from the others. Do not take anything for granted. Your customers will tell you what it is they want, if you will just ask. They will also tell you what else you can offer to fill their buying needs. This information often leads to new products, services and technologies. A commitment to continued improvement by asking your premier customer what they want will help you get **Top Dollar** for your product or service.

# CHAPTER THREE:
# THE CONTRACTOR'S PRIVATE
# ENTRANCE DOOR

### *How to create customer partnerships*

The sign on the side door of the doctor's office says *Private Entrance*. You have seen this, I'm sure. It is the door for your physician to come and go in a clandestine manner. Is the doctor the only one allowed through that door? Not usually. Employees, family and special guests are allowed through the door marked *Private Entrance.*

What would happen if your clients felt like they had a private entrance door to you, their contractor of choice? Of what value to your business would it be if every client you had felt like you were his or her partner? The notion of creating customer partnerships may be way out of your normal way of thinking. But just imagine for a moment if your physician allowed 'any-time access' through his private entrance door for you.

Seeing clients as partners rather than just customers or buyers of your service is an invaluable way of doing business. It is more economically rewarding. Mistakes or challenges in the partnership are more forgiving and the long-term relationship stays in tact. How do you create and maintain customer partnerships?

## A Matter of Attitude

The first step is to adopt the right attitude. Totally giving of yourself, your time, your energy, and your assets is the foundation for creating a client partnership. Your emphasis will be on fairness rather than equality. Compare it to a close friendship or well-adjusted marriage. There is plenty of give and more give before there is much taking.

The *"Private Entrance"* door means that your customer has total access to you, your time and to your talent. And of course, egos are left out in the hallway. I know the reality is you cannot be everywhere at once. Nor can you be everything to all of your clients. However, if your client perceives that you are really trying to be available to them, the psychological impact is tremendous.

Use all of the modern tools available to be accessible to your client partners. Voice mail messages can be updated daily. Give a brief overview of your daily schedule on the voice mail message, noting what times you may be available or at what time you will return calls. Return your calls at that time. Send an e-mail note acknowledging conversations with your client partners. Allow them to have your cell phone number, your pager number, your e-mail address or any other way to have access to you. Designate a person in your office to handle these calls if you need to. Let your client partner know exactly how to get in contact with you.

Now, some of you are saying, "My clients will never leave me alone to get anything done." That is not necessarily so. As in any respectful partnership, certain rules and guidelines are put into place early in the relationship. Predetermine when you will return calls and when you will have meetings with your client partner. Forthright conversations concerning these issues will set the partnership on the right course. I have known clients to greatly appreciate when I return their call just to say that I will talk to them later when I have more time to devote exclusively to their needs. They seem to appreciate the candor. This sort of courtesy pays big dividends. It is all a matter of attitude.

## Establish Mutual Goals

Knowing the ultimate outcome of the partnership is essential to building a rewarding partnership. When two people have a shared vision, the details of how to attain that vision seem to fall into place. In the very early stages of the partnership, learn exactly what the client wants. What is his or her ultimate goal in the project? Is it more space for the family? Must the project fit into an exact budget or is there a little latitude for upgrades? Are there time constraints? An open and honest assessment of what the exact desire of your client partner is will set the foundation for a profitable relationship.

Understand also that the finished product will satisfy some emotion for your client partner. Getting to know your client partner and learning their deep needs will help you to achieve your customer's aims and goals. Do not hesitate to ask specifically what they have in mind.

Now it is your turn. You also have goals. You have time of completion projections. You have quality and design goals. Obviously, there is a certain profit margin to be met. Stating out front what is included in your scope of work and what would be considered extra costs will reduce future tension. You also want to make your visions clear about what you consider to be a successful project. Convey to them the importance of time and budget for you as well. Today's client is very sophisticated. They understand costs and scheduling constraints more than you might expect.

After these discussions, determine the commonalties. Create a concise and memorable statement that reflects your mutual goals. If there are any issues or challenges during the project, the two of you can always reflect back on the mutually agreed mission of the project. The ultimate benefit of shared goals is that misunderstandings are reduced and each of you feels like the other's partner.

## *See Complaints as Gifts*

Invariably there will be issues that come up on your projects. Even with the best communication and a mutually shared vision, your customer will still see things from their perspective more than your viewpoint. It is human nature. What should you do when your customer complains and presents a challenge to you?

First, understand that a complaint can be turned into the gift of a learning opportunity. A complaint is not necessarily always a gripe about your work. It may be a sincere question that is asked in a misunderstood way. At the very worst, a complaint should be viewed as a challenge. Challenges are much easier to manage that problems or complaints. Complaints can be converted into an occasion to offer creative solutions.

I believe, in reality, clients do not expect you to be perfect. They do expect you to care enough to improve and to manage their concerns properly. Address the issue immediately, identify the challenge, understand the circumstances, and know all of the parties involved. Gather as much information as possible before taking corrective measures. Encourage your client partner to have an active role in the information gathering process. This process alone can help reduce your client's stress. Your client partners learn that you are genuinely interested; this is the foundation for setting up a solution.

Next, create a plan, or several plans, for the remedy. In all cases, get joint agreement on the solution and continue to communicate as it progresses. By all means, follow up with your client partner by making sure that the solution is satisfactory and that it meets the desired project outcomes for both of you.

There is one more thing. If you have a quiet client, consider that a dangerous thing. If you have set a good foundation with your client partner and then they seem to go into their pro-verbial cave, watch out. A quiet client is either not being candid with you; or you are not con-tacting them. He or she may be stewing about something. Some people may not complain to you, for a variety of reasons. However, they will tell their friends and associates at the drop of a hardhat. It is your job to do whatever it takes to get honest communication out of your client partner.

The bottom line is that client fulfillment is a matter of total commitment. You must be com-mitted to ongoing dialogue with your customer. Both of you must have the right attitude and a willingness to work through any issue pre-sented. In your pre-sale discussions with your prospective client partner, you must determine if this is a partnership that you want. Do this by taking the time to ask probing questions and finding out what the real expectations are of your prospective client partner. The client partnership format will give you a huge edge with your business.

Oh, about my doctor's *Private Entrance* door, I suppose some day I will be allowed access through the private entrance. Until then, I will just be another patient, another customer.

# CHAPTER FOUR:
# DEVELOP YOUR PERSONAL
# EXCELLENCE

## *Transform your life and your business*

There is a powerful shift taking place in this country regarding the long-term success of business. The traditional mindset of focusing only on increasing the size of your bank account is being counterbalanced with the importance of developing **Personal Excellence**. The premise: In order for your long-term business success to have a chance, your personal life skills must be in good shape.

In the construction business, this area is often neglected. Your personal foundation must be as strong as the foundations that support the buildings and homes you build. Personal excellence is attained with your dedication to constant and never ending improvement in every area of life. It involves a resolution to search out new and advanced ways to expand your individual identity and refine your personal skills.

Dedicating time to be in the **Personal Excellence Gymnasium** will have a transforming effect on your life and your business. The most successful individuals in society are those living a balanced life. Here are the three primary areas on which to focus in the pursuit of personal excellence.

## *Personal Balance*

Balance must be attained with the condition of your mental, emotional, spiritual, and physical health. The balancing act can be tricky. These areas are so closely related to each other that when one is out of balance, all are effected. For example, when you experience mental anguish because one of your customers is withholding your final draw, you may feel sluggish or exhibit flu-like symptoms. Similarly, when your pollen allergies are acting up, your mental focus is not as sharp as usual. Scientific research is overwhelming when it comes to the connection between the mind and the body.

Add to this the fact that events in life occur that creates imbalance. This is part of the natural ebb and flow of life. The commitment to **Personal Excellence** requires an ongoing awareness of what is working and what areas need help.

You probably already have a good idea of what works for you in your life in order to have personal balance. The question is ... Are you taking action on what you know? There is no need to wait until the agony of being out of balance forces you to take action. If one area of your life is out of whack, it may require some concentrated effort to bring it up to the level of the other areas.

Perhaps, you have been so busy working that you have neglected your physical conditioning. Or, maybe you have spent so much energy protecting your money and personal assets that you have missed opportunities to contribute your time, resources, and expertise. Philanthropic gestures help create genuine balance in your life.

Do not lose hope or get dejected. I recommend that you get life coaching or private counseling from someone who excels in the area in which you are lacking. Consider this an investment in your personal balance. Often, just an honest appraisal and your dedication to take action will set you on the right course back to personal balance.

I don't believe there is such a thing as "once balanced, always balanced." Staying balanced is an ongoing, conscious activity that rounds out your life and allows you to be the best contractor and best person that you can possibly be.

## *Communication Skills*

Your ability to effectively communicate and build lasting rapport with people will transform your life and your business. Your level of **Personal Excellence** can be greatly increased with your commitment to improving the quality of your communication.

Do you want to get full price for your service or product? If your answer is yes, your communication skills must continue to improve. Your ability to demonstrate that you are honest, trustworthy and that you are serving the needs of your client is in direct proportion to the bottom line on your profit and loss statement.

You would think this is a no-brainer. However, a lack of quality communication continues to be the most common reason for customer challenges in the construction industry.

The best way to be an effective communicator is to remove your ego from your interactions with others. In other words, you must be totally present and attentive with your clients, vendors, employees, and trade contractors. Removing your ego doesn't mean that you let go of your personal confidence. It simply means that you are more interested in the other person than you are in your own personal agenda. You will certainly maintain your vested interest in the conversations and interaction you have with other people. However, when you remove your personal issues and operate from a service mentality, it allows you to be a more effective communicator.

Having good communication skills relates to personal balance. When your life is out of balance, you tend to bring that baggage to work. It adversely affects your employees, clients, and everyone around you. Instead of listening to the needs of your employees and clients, you may be using them for your personal therapy. This may sound like a tough statement. However, if you frequently have challenges with people, take a closer look at your style of communication. Ask and answer the following questions to get a sense of your effectiveness as a communicator.

1.  Do I frequently repeat what I say so that others get my point?

2.  Do I catch myself daydreaming or mentally drifting into space when talking to someone?

3.  Am I thinking about the next thing to say or do when someone is talking to me?

4.  Do others express frustration because I tend to forget the details of the conversation?

5.  Do I get frustrated because people just don't understand me?

6. Would I rather not talk at all, in order to avoid confusion?

7. Do I interrupt conversations in order to get my two cents worth in?

8. Do others feel refreshed and uplifted after talking to me?

9. Am I able to end a conversation feeling good about what has been said?

10. Do I think that everyone else has a communication problem?

11. Am I able to get agreement from others to take action after a conversation?

12. Do people disappear when I enter a room?

13. Is my conversation time with others an equally shared experience?

14.   Do I look forward to conversations with customers, employees, trade contractors and vendors?   Or do I just avoid them all together?

15.   Would I rather spend time alone than have the hassles of talking to someone else?

16.   Do I get my feelings hurt easily and regularly?

17.   Do I judge others before they finish their conversation?

If the answers to any of the above questions plague you, get help.   Attend a communication workshop.   Pick up a book or audio CD on the subject of communication.   Feel free to request my 55-minute audio CD, "The Message is You; The Art of Persuasive Communication."   This CD will teach you key foundational strategies for positive communication.   Or just have a true friend be candid with you about your communication style. If communication is stressful, do something about it.

Acquiring personal balance allows you to focus on the needs and desires of those with whom you interact. Listening to, and acknowledging the other person validates their worth. It puts you in control of the outcome and sets you both up for an "everyone wins" transaction.

An additional benefit is that when you communicate effectively, your client will understand the enormous value of your product and your service. They will pay full price and they will also reward you with repeat business and direct referral leads for new customers. And that translates into improved profit power.

## *Invest In Yourself*

In order to have personal balance and exquisite communication skills, you must invest in yourself. Your excellence expands every time you invest in your personal development. Notice that I refer to this strategy as an investment. There is no amount of money that is too much for your own personal growth. As you budget in physical food, factor into your budget mental and emotional food.

There are many ways to do this. Attend a personal development seminar. Listen to communication skills CD's. Read autobiographies of successful people. Watch inspirational videotapes. Create or join a mastermind group. Hire a personal or professional "life coach." Volunteer your time and expertise to a worthy cause for those less fortunate in your community. The point is to do something and do it on a regular basis. Continually investing in your personal worth will pay huge dividends in your personal life and in your business. Make a commitment today to put yourself in the **Personal Excellence Gymnasium** on a regular basis.

This is an area about which I am most passionate. My articles, books and audio series regularly emphasize business success strategies for today's contractor. In addition, I am certain that all of the business strategies in the world don't mean a thing if your life is a mess. I believe that your long-term business success is directly related to your commitment to **Personal Excellence**. There is no separation of the two.

It may be challenging at times. It may not seem as though one relates to the other. It may mean taking an honest look at yourself. It may not seem like you are making progress at times. However, when you make a decision to put yourself in the **Personal Excellence Gymnasium** and work at it consistently, the muscles get stronger and more defined. I also believe that anything you set your mind to do will take place, if you just allow it.

# CHAPTER FIVE:
# THINKING OUTSIDE THE SALE

### *You may not be having enough fun*

I received a call recently from a design/build-remodeling contractor on the East Coast. I detected by the tone in his voice that he was fairly stressed out about his recent lack of sales success. He complained that his closing ratios were way down compared to last year and that his prospective customers seemed really tense about the economy and life in general.

He said he had as many or more leads as the same time last year. And the projects he was selling were about the same size as this time last year. According to him, all things seemed equal in his business except he wasn't closing as many deals.

With some further questioning, I found out that about 6 months prior to his call to me he began to change his selling strategies. He had made a conscious decision to increase his sales to grow his company larger. "Everything seems right with that concept," I thought. However, when he began to press harder to increase his sales, he noticed his stress level rise and he wasn't having as much fun selling his services.

And I thought to myself ... Therein lies the answer to his challenges. He wasn't having as much fun as he had in the past.

I will get back to his story in a minute.

First, understand that selling can sometimes be a tricky deal. Do you ever really know what the prospect is thinking? Sometimes you do, but usually it is a guessing game. They are trying to figure out you and your motives while you are doing the same with them.

As in the case of the contractor from the East Coast, he was over-thinking his sales strategies and techniques. I found out later in the conversation the biggest reason he had sales success in the past is that his customers really liked him, they trusted him and they all said working with him was a pleasant experience because he was so friendly and easy to get along with.

And then he changed.

By his own admission he got "deadly" serious about selling. In the sales seminars he was taking, he was taught the seven steps to closing. He was being taught how to assess different personality styles and how to sell to each of them. He was focusing on a systematic disciplined way to close deals. He was being taught that selling is a serious business and there were specific steps that he must follow or he would fail. He bought into the program and he was giving it his best effort.

While I certainly subscribe to the philosophies of many selling courses, most of them seem to leave out one single major component. That component is to have fun with the process. I am not talking about being a prankster or comedian. I am talking about being your natural, jovial, friendly self.

It was obvious by our further conversation that this is not a "deadly" serious guy. He really gets a kick out of life and I suspect that his customers enjoy dealing with a person of that demeanor. I will tell you later what he did to remedy his challenge.

You want to know what I think is the biggest problem with sales people?

They are way too serious for what they are selling. They get out of their natural character when they are selling. They are not authentic. They talk way too much and they are not genuinely interested in their prospect. You think your prospect doesn't detect your insincerity and that you are out of character? They may not know it, but they can feel it "in their bones."

What do you really have to lose by being yourself in front of your customer?

The United States of America is the richest country in the world. Americans have homes that are ten or twenty times larger than the average home of most of the populated world. You drive cars that are fancier than... well, actually a huge percentage of the globe's population walk everywhere they go.

And what about the food you eat? Well, it doesn't get any more abundant than here in the United States of America.

You don't mind going out on the weekend and having a great time at the ballgame or at a dance. You can joke and cut up with your friends until the laughter makes you cry. But when it comes to selling, it is like the solemn walk to death row for most people. They put on a game face that repels prospective customers.

Do you want to explode your sales to a whole new higher level? Get your prospect to laugh, or at least smile a lot.

Now I am not suggesting that you go into your next sales call acting like Gallagher or Jim Carey. (That is unless you really do have a personality like those jokesters).

What I am saying is lighten up. Have a little fun with your job. People love to do business with people they like. And most of your customers like people who are fun, interesting and optimistic.

Could you repeat a funny story you heard Paul Harvey report? Could you clip out a funny comic strip that relates to your business? Or would you have the guts to say a little something

funny or even slightly embarrassing about yourself?

Could you at least have a huge sincere smile
when you greet your prospect? This is not nuclear physics, folks. Let your genuine personality come out and have a little fun when selling.

It has been said that laughter can heal the
sick. Could laughter or lightheartedness heal
your ailing sales success? Did you know that
you have eighty muscles in your face? At any
given moment, you can lift your facial muscles
up toward the sky, create a grin and instantly
feel better. Your facial muscles can send a sig-
nal to your brain that you are happy and feeling
optimistic. That optimism can put your brain in
a more creative mode, allowing you to come up
with all sorts of answers to help your prospective
client buy from you.

My advice is for you to lighten up. Sure, this is a serious business, but it also can be a very fulfilling business, if you just allow it to.

Let's get back to the contractor from the East Coast. He called me about a week later and said he closed a big deal that he had been working on for three months. "What prompted your customer to buy?" I quizzed. He said that he sent his prospect a greeting card with a frizzy haired, bulging eyeballed, scientist looking character on the front of the card. The inside of the card said, "I have been stressed out and going crazy cause I haven't heard from you lately." He enclosed his business card and then waited.

Three days later, he received a phone call from his prospective client saying they wanted to talk to him again about the project. By his own admission, his renewed frame of mind put him in a more positive state and allowed him to come up with some creative solutions to make the project fit into his prospect's budget.

In order to increase your profit power, sometimes you have to think outside the sale to make the sale.

# CHAPTER SIX:
# WHY HURRY UP AND WAIT ?

### *Make the bidding process work for you*

Do you ever feel like the bidding process is nothing more than a "hurry up and wait" game? It rarely happens that your first meeting with a prospective client results in a signed contract or work order, especially when a sizable project and large investment is at stake. More often, you are invited to preview a project and then asked to turn in the bid at a later date. Many times, your bid is turned in two, three, or four weeks later, and sometimes even longer. This is a result of the natural process of obtaining trade contractor sub bids and material bids. You then must compile these, add them up, and formulate your proposal for submission.

In the meantime, other bidders come along and tend to "muddy the waters." They may give information contrary to what you have given your prospective client. The other bidders may make claims or promises that sound better than yours. At the very least, their presence is the most recent in the mind of your prospect.

How can you manage the bidding process so that you maintain an ongoing presence with the prospect? Here are several ways to build the relationship with the prospect while their bid proposal is being prepared.

## *The $3.49 Solution*

The final set of contract specifications is rarely the first set presented to a prospective client. Offering a set of preliminary specifications in advance of the final contract document can have many advantages.

While the final drafts are being prepared, what would happen if you sent a "rough draft" copy to the prospect? Walk, run, drive, or beam yourself up to the nearest office supply store and invest $3.49 in a "ROUGH DRAFT" rubber stamp. On every proposal that you submit prior to the final agreement, conspicuously stamp "ROUGH DRAFT."

By presenting a "rough draft" copy of specifications, you begin to educate your prospect about the way that your company does business. It prepares the client for what they can look forward to in the final copy of contract specifications. A dialogue with the prospect is now opened as they study the "rough draft" copy. This dialogue can be extremely valuable. The prospect may reveal additional information that would be critical to the price. They may have certain expectations of you, the contractor, that otherwise would not have been mentioned. You begin to learn more about the way your prospective client does business and also what past experiences they have had with other projects.

All of these bits and pieces of information begin to add up to something of value. You may get an edge with your pricing. You may find out what their budget is for the project or how they intend to finance the project. An atmosphere of trust begins to develop as the relationship grows. Your prospect begins to reason that you are dealing with them as a true professional and the value of your service is worth the investment they will make.

A "ROUGH DRAFT" rubber stamp is a small investment that can pay huge dividends. It allows you the opportunity to stay in contact with your prospective customer while engaged in the bidding process. The optimal way to use the $3.49 "ROUGH DRAFT" rubber stamp strategy is to dribble out information to your prospective customer a little at a time. Keep them engaged and interested in the bidding process. It builds anticipation and demonstrates to your prospective customer that you will pay attention to detail. Paying attention to the details of the proposal during the bidding process sends a message to your prospect that you will do the same when the project is awarded to you.

## *Offer Options*

The time you spend with your prospect in advance of your final bid submission can create additional profit opportunities. Often, a prospective client will disclose new information about upgrades or change orders that they would be willing to consider. You may learn that they have discovered these options from other bidders. That can be a very valuable piece of information during the bidding process.

You now have learned that your prospect is willing to accept other ideas. You may offer additional services that the prospect had not originally thought about. You may come up with other creative ways to perform the actual project. You certainly can offer alternative estimates for a variety of projects related to the original bid. The fact that you even present these options to your prospect indicates that you, too, are value and cost conscious.

When working with large investments like homes, remodeling projects and major construction work, most people like many options. The more options you offer the better. The more information that you give your prospect, the more informed they are to buy from you. Don't think for a moment that your prospective customer won't find out about all the alternatives in their project. There is too much information available for them on the Internet and in the media. If they are serious buyers, they will find out what they need. Position yourself as the resource to give them all the options they want.

Here is a point about offering pricing options. Pricing options need to be set in front of a potential client to emphasize the value of what you will do for your customer. Options should be presented in a way that add greater value to your original proposal. After reviewing the options you have presented, your prospective client will have no other alternative than to award you the contract.

To increase your profit power, pricing options should be offered in a clear and understandable way. Start with a base price and then add your pricing options as though you are climbing a ladder. The larger services and larger pricing options will be offered last. Also, do comparative pricing options. In other words, if an additional 500-sq. ft. of space will cost $50,000, offer a comparative price for 600-sq. ft. at $65,000. Though, your prospective customer may not have asked for the 600-sq. ft. price, the comparison can help them solidify the 500-sq.ft. price option.

With the proliferation of creative financing programs, you must also be ready to offer a wide variety of financing plans. Do your homework and create alliances with lending institutions so that you are educated on what is available in the market. Offering financing options to your pro- spective customer demonstrates your knowledge of the business and also shows your willingness to help.

Your knowledge of the options alone will sometimes endorse you as the expert. These strategies will continue to build the value of your service in the mind of your prospect. Offering options to the original bid request may pique the interest of your prospect enough to allow you to extend the bid submission date in order to pro- vide more accurate bid information or better products.

These are not delay tactics, rather they are value-building strategies. The competition is fierce and you need something to set you apart. Why not take a little extra time and be more thorough than your competition? When pricing is very close, these concepts can be the difference in having a contract awarded or not.

## *Other Benefits*

Using the interim time period during the bidding process wisely can benefit you in other ways. It affords you the opportunity to "multi-task." That is, you can work on several bids simultaneously. Your pricing of the final specifications is more precise and there is less chance for error.

Once the prospective client accepts the proposal, the time it takes to mobilize your trade contractors and vendors is greatly reduced. This will generate even better customer service and increase your profit power.

Another very important aspect of this strategy is that it allows you to get to know your prospective customer better. A serious buyer will welcome any and all pre-bid communication.

They want a successful project and will usually take the time in advance of the project to work out the questions and anxieties they may be experiencing.

The bottom line of these strategies is that it builds the relationship with the prospect and it gives you an ongoing presence with them. When the prospect feels that their relationship with you has been built due to your diligence and interest in the project, it may mean that you are awarded the contract without hesitation. It also means that the bidding process is working for you and that you don't have to "hurry up and wait."

## Chapter Seven:

# HOW TO MAXIMIZE YOUR PUBLICITY

### *Top 10 list of low or no-cost marketing*

Marketing and publicity are the driving force behind every viable business. After all, if your potential clients do not know that you exist, how can they become your clients? Multi-billionaire Donald Trump says, *"the only bad publicity is no publicity."* Well, with some of the publicity he has had over the years, I am not sure I completely agree with that. The point is, everyone knows of Trump and something about his business.

The benefits of publicity are enormous. When massive amounts of people know who you are, what your product or service is, and how it can benefit them, your chance of obtaining new clients dramatically increases. The challenge is that fancy ad campaigns, marketing research and publicity agents can represent a sizable investment. There are times when these resources may be appropriate. For most contractors though, the best kind of publicity is *FREE PUBLICITY,* or at least very low cost publicity. Here are the top ten ideas and resources about obtaining *FREE PUBLICITY* that I have collected over the years that will benefit your company.

## 1. Join organizations and associations and get involved.

Become an active member in the organizations that represent your industry. Speak on behalf of the organization to consumer groups and potential clients. Do this for free and with no hidden agenda of obtaining business, but rather as open information to benefit the public.

Get on boards of directors and committees in your association. You can have a visible presence in the community when you serve on com-

mittees or when you are on the board of directors. It may require that you plan your schedule
much more carefully, but it will be worth the effort.

Representing your industry association as a
director also positions you as a dedicated expert
in your field. The public at large will tend to
view you as a leader and will turn to you for
business. It also helps you to stay focused and
grounded in the industry of your choice.

## 2.   Get involved in lateral organizations.

Lateral organizations are those which trade
or sell to the construction industry. By joining
and getting involved in organizations that support the construction industry, your network of
meaningful contacts will expand.

Banking, real estate, and insurance adjuster
associations are a natural support to your industry. Your presence and expertise will be a

tremendous asset to these organizations. This will lead to more business from sources you may not have consciously targeted.

As with construction industry associations, you must get involved in these lateral associations. To be a member, paying membership dues and simply showing up at the monthly meetings is not enough. If you want to get business referrals from the businesses that support your industry, you must have an active role in the association. Choose the association or associations that best fit your career track. Also, if you want leads and referrals, be willing and ready to provide plenty of leads and referrals to the members of these lateral associations.

### 3.   Send out press releases.

Press releases should be a regular part of your marketing plan. This low cost strategy is one of the most effective ways to get free publicity. All it takes is a word processing program, a printer and a fax machine. Beware. You won't be the only one sending a press release to the media. Even so, you will be one of the few contractors that send out press releases.

A press release should only be one page in length. It should have the title at the top of the page that says, "FOR IMMEDIATE RELEASE." The subject line to follow must have a catchy phrase and offer the element of intrigue. For example, one of my builder clients wanted to send out a notice to the media of an upcoming trade show booth. This particular booth was larger than usual and had some very creative elements to it.

The builder was a newly formed team of father and son. The son had recently joined his father in the business after obtaining a Masters Degree in marketing. We crafted the subject line to say, "SON MAKES FATHER PROUD. FINALLY!"

They got good response from the media and had a successful trade show.

After an intriguing subject line, you must get to the point immediately and let the press know when, where, why, who, and the dates of the event. Send notices of changes or improvements in your business. Announce new employees, project awards, community support projects, certifications, and office relocations. You can send press releases to industry trade journals, local newspapers, association newsletters and corresponding associations. Always mention your company name and a brief comment about your service or product along with your current contact information.

## 4. Teach a class.

Continuing education classes for school districts and community colleges provide an opportunity to share your business knowledge and experience with others. By teaching, you will gain credibility as an established expert in your community. Your educational colleagues and students will share your experiences with others.

You can teach business topics, financial topics, project management topics, or technical topics. If you own a family structured business, teach family business skills.

In all cases, send out press release notices of your classes. Save student testimonials, course certifications and public notices to put in your marketing kit.

## 5.    Form alliances.

There are many companies and individuals with which you should partner. With partners you gain all of their partners. Partners and alliances multiply your impact in the market.

You can create alliances with lending institutions, Chambers of Commerce, trade show exhibitors, schools, universities, associations, and many more. The objective is creating a win/win relationship where both parties gain market impact and increase their business opportunities.

One of the best ways to form an alliance is to act as a sub contractor or joint venture with other contractors when possible. In order to take on larger jobs, you may consider this. Your partner's clients, in effect, become yours, and vice versa.

Join or create a mastermind or "think tank" in the local community. When business associates from different industries group together in a mastermind arrangement, it can open opportunities for all involved. This support system can be used to collaborate on marketing programs and advertising campaigns.

Create alliances with your trade contractors. Get them involved in your marketing campaigns and ask them to supply co-operative dollars for more aggressive marketing. Your trade contractors can partner with you at trade shows so that you have more booth space. Your trade contractors can partner with you to co-sponsor community support events.

Every professional contact you have can be a potential partner. There is strength in numbers and the more alliances you have, the more your marketing dollar will stretch.

## 6. Ask! That's right. Ask!

Did I say ask? I made this point in my first book, *101 Power Strategies; Tools to Promote Yourself as the Contractor of Choice.* A builder from Texas called me one day to say that he read the book and employed two of the strategies immediately. The very next week he signed a $258,000 contract with a remodeling customer. He did Strategy #1, "Talk to Everyone You Know" and Strategy #3, "Ask, Ask, Ask." That is not bad for a $17 investment.

Sometimes, you just get so bogged down with work that you forget the simple things. Asking for business is one of the oldest, simplest, most fundamental ways of growing your enterprise. Yet, it is the one that is frequently overlooked. It just seems too elementary.

Ask for at least 3 leads from every client and provide a self-addressed, stamped envelope for their convenience. Reward them for the new business you obtain from their referral. Regarding rewards for your customers, I have known of contracts that included a clause requiring at least three legitimate referrals. Incentives for customer referrals make asking for leads much more appealing to you. Keep a tickler file for re-contacting your clients every 3 to 6 months. Re-connect the relationship with them and ask again for their business or if they know of someone who needs your service.

Ask for leads from your banker, CPA, insurance agent, barber, massage therapist, ticket broker, mechanic, shoe shine man, trade contractors, employees, vendors, colleagues, Mayor, Realtor, and your kid's teachers. You get the point. Ask for business and business leads from everyone you know.

Ask, ask, and ask. Did I say ask?

## 7. Be a radio or TV resource.

Offer your expertise and experience to a radio or TV show when there is a newsworthy item related to your business. For example, an HVAC contractor may offer 5 simple steps for keeping your house cool and energy efficient in the hot summer months. A builder can speak about the advantages of environmentally responsible green building. A remodeling contractor may offer expert advice about maintenance tips to protect the appraised value of a home.

Becoming a resource to the media requires dedication and commitment. The payoff is huge.

If you can get interviewed on TV or the radio, literally thousands of eyes and ears will be tuned in. As a media resource, you must be available all the time. Give them your cell phone number or a number where you can be reached immediately. If you are not available the reporter will move on to the next industry expert, which will likely be your competition. Understand that news reporters are very busy. They want small bites of information relative to hot issues. Keep your comments short and to the point. Answer questions directly and expand on your topic only when asked. Tailor your contribution to what is current in the news.

How do you get started to position yourself as a media resource? It frequently starts with the press release strategy mentioned earlier in this chapter. Frequent, consistent press releases sent to media outlets lets them know that you are an expert and available. You should also be on the watch for current events that relate to your business. When you see such an event, call the radio station or TV station and offer your advice and opinion.

This strategy doesn't cost anything other than your time and energy. It can actually be fun and exciting if you choose. And the impression you make in the media can have long-range benefits for the profit power of your business.

## 8.   Have stuff and label your stuff.

"Stuff" is the loose language I use to refer to all of your promotional material.   Promotional material can be anything from printed paper to truck signage to coffee mugs and key chains. Your promotional material should be with you at all times. Make it a habit to carry your brochure, one-page ad, and promotional packet.   Include in them awards and any recognition you have received.

Put your company name and critical information on your stuff. Make sure your contact information, that is, telephone number and website address, are conspicuously displayed on your stuff. Let others know who you are and what qualifies you as an expert. Label everything from your trucks and cars to your pens and pencils. Be proud of your promotional stuff. I affectionately call it in my business the, "We love us package."

## 9.   Have a super Website.

Hellooooooo!   If you do not have a website yet, here is a suggestion for your domain address; www.WelcomeToTheNewMillenium.com.   I joke.   However, as I travel through the country and deliver seminars to contractor groups, my informal surveys show that only about 35% of contractors have a website.   Of that 35%, only about 10% say that they get regular leads and business referrals from their website.   The first printing of this book is being published in 2003 and I am amazed at the lack of commitment to having an Internet presence.

I am certain that many contractors are misinformed about the cost of creating a well-developed website. Let me put your mind to rest. You can get a pretty nice website for around $500. It won't be very big, but you will have an Internet presence. You can get a dynamic website for about $5,000. It is up to you.

Today's consumer is so sophisticated. They are so knowledgeable and product savvy. How did they get that way? The Internet is one primary way. Don't you shop online? I do. Your customers do. The Internet is here to stay. It is not the future. It is NOW. Your customer can find out everything about you and your business before they ever call your office or send you an email. Help them out. Help them find out what you want them to know about you.

There are three levels of websites for contractors. Determine the level that is right for you and make a commitment to expand your Internet presence each year.

Level One: "Brochure Style." This is a simple website with just three to five pages. It is an electronic brochure. It consists of basic facts about your company, your expertise, and your contact information. It may have a few graphics of your projects or photos of the owners of the company. Its purpose is to serve as an entry-level site.

Level Two: "Intermediate Style." This is a more advanced website with multiple pages. Ten to fifteen pages are common on this site. It includes more information like testimonials, contact pages, staff biographies, frequently asked questions (FAQ), consumer tips, advice columns and helpful links. It usually has more photos of projects and usually includes your company logo and artwork. Its purpose is to engage the visitor and this site is more informational in nature.

Level Three: "Advanced Style." This is a very advanced, dynamic site. It has all of the components of level two, and then some. The main feature of the site is that it is highly graphic oriented. It has many project photos, awards photos, client testimonial pictures, and portfolio information. It usually includes a downloadable .pdf brochure or information packet. It educates the prospective customer about how to buy from you. A unique feature of this very advanced contractor website is a project management page. The customer can log into a private, password-protected area of the website and get an update on their project in progress. This is an award-winning site.

You can have any or all of the features mentioned above. A bona fide Internet presence requires your commitment to your website and its ongoing development.

## 10. Email Correspondence

This is a very low cost way of maintaining a presence in front of your clients. Your email correspondence can act as an advertisement every time you hit the send button. Most email programs allow you, the sender, to put a "signature" at the end of your outgoing emails. Include your name, your company name, contact information and your website address. You do have a website, don't you? See #9 above. It also can include a very short version of your company's value statement.

You also can send out regular email correspondence in the form of a newsletter or broadcast. These are two primary ways to communicate with your client via email. Each has a specific purpose and you determine the frequency of each.

"Email Newsletter". They are just what it says. The newsletter only needs to be a couple of hundred words long. Brevity is important. It must have a tip or provide something of value. It must be more than just junk mail. Always offer a product or service at the end of the newsletter and a way for the newsletter to be subscribed to by others. It is sent out on a regular basis, usually once a quarter, once a month or bi-monthly. It can be text or html. HTML is a graphics oriented newsletter. For a sample of an html newsletter, sign up for my free bi-monthly newsletter at www.ContractorOfChoice.com.

"Email Broadcast". These are event-driven email notices to your clients. It announces special offers, awards recognition, new projects for sale, etc. Its purpose is to keep your customer informed about late breaking news and to give you special one-time promotion. It is sent only as often as you have special announcements.

## *Publicity Summary*

As you might have noticed, publicity is one of my favorite topics. Publicity for your business is an ongoing venture. Investing the time and energy in these small ways can pay huge dividends when building a client base. One note of encouragement is to FOLLOW UP. Whatever leads for potential new business come your way needs to follow up so they can become deals and increase your profit power.

# CHAPTER EIGHT:
# "ALL SYSTEMS GO"

## *Run your business instead of your business running you*

"There just isn't enough time in the day to get it all done." "If I had an additional four hours or just one extra day each week, maybe I could get more done." This is the sentiment of many business owners. One of the most common challenges facing construction entrepreneurs in this economy is the difficulty of doing everything needed to maintain and manage the business.

In the beginning of your business venture the majority of your effort is spent promoting and marketing in hopes of obtaining enough business to get free time to enjoy life. The irony for many entrepreneurs is the more clients and revenue you generate, the more time and effort it takes to manage the business.

What is the answer? *Systems* need to be in place to help your business run more smoothly and efficiently. *A system is the disciplined arrangement of actions taken to allow specific areas of your business to operate with minimal control on your part.* In other words, a standard operating procedure (SOP) is predetermined and tested to ensure that quality, productivity, accountability, and profitability are maintained.

The SOP can be set in place for any segment of your business. It should be a clearly written set of instructions for each function of your business and maintained in an electronic format or in a three-ring binder. A written set of instructions is extremely important.

Here are seven reasons to put your standard operating procedures in writing and keep them in a specific electronic document or three-ring binder.

1. Clarity. Writing out the procedure allows you to think through the process more clearly. When you write out the system, you have a better opportunity to clarify the specific steps required for making your systems work. You also can focus more on what is important in a specific process and what is not needed.

2. Accessibility. Keeping your non-confidential systems in a three-ring binder allows everyone in your operation to have access to policies and procedures. Confidential systems should be kept in a safe or locked cabinet and only the personnel that are authorized have access to those procedures. The electronic equivalent of your three-ring binder should also be kept in an appropriate—accessible or secure— location in your computer.

3. Organization. The process of putting the system in writing is a system itself. Organizing your systems on a regular basis force you to continuously look for better and more efficient ways to perform. Clutter is distracting and leads to confusion. When your standard operating procedures are organized it becomes easier to work more efficiently and profitably.

4. Flexibility. When there are changes or modifications to a specific system, it is easier to add your documentation to the three-ring binder or to change your electronic files. By definition, a system is designed to bring discipline to a specific process. The reality is that changes are inevitable and you need the flexibility to make alterations.

5. Transferability. When you have personnel changes, the next person can transition into the system much quicker, easier and

with far less confusion. When you want to delegate tasks or responsibility, your SOP is easily transferable.

6. Consistency. Systemization of your procedures clearly defines expectations for your employees and staff. Your clients will receive consistent, high quality service. Your employees will experience less stress when they are clear about their responsibilities.

7. Accountability. A standard operating procedure clearly directs who is responsible for specific activities in your company. Placing unjustified blame for work not performed or work performed poorly will be a thing of the past. The responsible parties will be easily identifiable.

Policies and standard operating procedures can, and should, be created for virtually every area of your business. Here are just a few areas for which you should consider creating a system.

- Marketing frequency and targeted demographics

- Sales leads, sales appointments, sales tracking

- Loan processing and funding after a sale is made

- Customer product selections

- Building production, job scheduling and punch lists

- Accounting, payroll, accounts payable and receivables

- Hiring, orientation and training new staff, performance reviews

- On-site project management

- Off-site project management

- Safety, ethics and customer responsiveness

- Purchasing non project related items, e.g. office supplies

- Product order fulfillment, invoicing and payments

- Warranty service, customer satisfaction

- Project follow up surveys and project debriefing

As you can see, there are many areas in which your business can have a set of disciplined standard operating procedures. Must every area of your business have a specific set of systematic procedures to follow? The answer is simple. The more areas that have a standard operating procedure, the more efficiently your enterprise will run. That means less frustration for you and more profit power for your company.

You may wonder how to set up systems in your business. I want to give you a few fundamental suggestions for getting started with creating systems. Understand that you can begin small and build upon your experience and your success. Eventually, you will be able to create systems in a rapid manner and they will work more efficiently for you.

Here are three basic steps for creating systems in your business.

## *Set up the System*

Identify one specific function of your business and examine closely what happens in that area. Ask yourself, "What is the natural and logical order of things to be done?" Start with the most basic step needed. Do not assume anything. If a phone call is involved in the process, make note of that. If a form or some paperwork is required, make note of that. Which employees, trade contractors, or vendors are involved in this function? Examine the entire process of that one area from start to finish. With each step in the process, record precisely what is happening. Documentation is essential.

The objective here is to identify every detail of the process and record these details. You will begin to arrange a blueprint of the system and the procedures involved. Keep in mind that once the system is created; it should be transferable to virtually anyone who comes to work for you. It is imperative that the details of the function be noted in order for other people to understand the entire process of the function. The system will run the business and the people in your business will run the system.

## *Test the System*

Now that you have a written record of the steps required for a specific function in your business, test the process. In other words, run the operation exactly as you have it documented.

Do not deviate. The concept here is for anyone to be able to read the steps, follow them and obtain the desired end result.

During this testing period, notice what is working and what needs to be refined. Ask for feedback from those involved in the particular function you are testing. Remember the goal is for the written process to be easy to duplicate many times with the same effective, efficient results. If there is a step that is not working or seems out of order, correct it and document it. The system should be tested enough times for there to be a standard operating procedure established.

Is this operating procedure set up in such a way that people can easily be trained in the system? The documentation may need to be revised in order to create clarity for your people. Now test the system again by training someone else to perform the operation. If the trainee is able to perform the process and the desired end result is obtained, then your system is in good shape.

## *Refine the System*

Once you have a system in place with a set of written guidelines, look for ways to improve the system. This usually becomes apparent when the system fails or does not work up to its potential. The addition of new products or services may require refinement of the system or may create a need for a whole new system.

The hiring of new employees or technological advances may dictate a change in your systems. An increase in your sales volume may mean that your system needs to be refined. Or you may just think of a different and better way to perform a certain procedure.

The ideal system will allow for changes in your business. However, the reality is, as your business changes so must your systems. It's not something you do and then are done with. It's something you do all the time. With the innovation of new products and services, your systems continue to be refined.

The benefits of setting up systems in your business are enormous. Consider these benefits.

- Your people will run the systems that run your business. This will empower your staff to make decisions more freely based on the systems in place.

- It will allow you time to focus your energy on the expansion, recognition, and perpetuity of your enterprise. You will also have time for more creative thoughts about growing your business.

- Your business is not dependent on any particular person. In the case of an emergency or loss of personnel, your systems allow your operation to continue more smoothly.

- It is easier to hire new staff. Once the system is created, you can hire based on the functions of the system. With specific systems in place it is easier to create job descriptions and to match new staff with their particular strengths.

- Systems guide your daily actions and help you stay on task and not feel so fragmented. Standard operating systems create an easier environment to be more disciplined with your daily tasks.

- Your employees and customers will know exactly what to expect from your business and the system. Expectations, goals, objectives and outcomes are clearly defined and remove guesswork. An environment of certainty is put in place.

- You will be in charge of your business rather than your business running you. The biggest benefit of creating standard operating systems is that you maintain control of your business. You do not operate in a crisis management mode.

- Systems allow you to measure success in your business. Standard operating procedures are more disciplined by definition. Disciplines are easier to measure and correct when something goes array.

- Standard operating procedures allow everyone in your company to be on the same page. Systems create a common direction and it becomes easier for your staff to follow the direction provided by your systems.

- Unity of purpose and process creates a tighter bond in your team. Team unity is critical and standard operating procedures give your team a sense of purpose to accomplish common goals.

- Systems prevent you from having to micromanage your people. Systems allow you to remove yourself from the minute to minute managing of your people. Your staff is empowered to be creative and to think on their own to support the systems.

- Standard operating procedures prevent you from being in a reactive or crisis management mode all the time. Tested standard operating systems tend to remove unexpected events. Systems provide you the opportunity to anticipate changes and give you the freedom to operate without fear of changes.

The bottom line is that a systematic approach to the processes and functions in your business will increase your profit power, and, isn't that what you really want?

# CHAPTER NINE:
# TEAMING UP FOR SUCCESS

## *Building a dynamic team of people to support you*

"It is so hard to find good help and to keep good people on staff." This is the most common challenge I hear from contractors around the country. The unemployment rate in 2003 is at its lowest levels in decades. As a result, employees and sub-contractors move from one company to the next at a gypsy-like pace. Contractors remain in a search for quality employees and trade contractors to bring on board.

In this chapter, you will learn how the top contractors in the country are able to keep their team together. Two key areas will be discussed. First, you will take a look at how to retain quality employees. Then you will see how to keep your skilled trade contractors motivated and in-spired to produce high quality work for you.

## *Keep your employees happy*

The first order of business is to eliminate the term employee from your vocabulary. Refer to your people as associates, team members, part-ners, staff or "super people." The point is that you must elevate their position to much more than a wage-earning, clock-punching employee. Choose an empowering term for your team and have them take ownership of that term. In one of my companies, we affectionately refer to our team as "the posse." It may not be all that unique, but it works for us.

Take a look at the top ten things employers must do to retain employees in their company. This will give you insight to keep your quality employees happy, motivated, productive, and working to increase your profit power.

1. **Define expectations and outcomes clearly.** The most satisfied employees know exactly what is expected of them and what the ultimate outcome is of a particular project or job description. In other words, they know what the big picture is for their position. Most importantly, they have managers or employers that allow them to find their own route toward those outcomes. The best employers know and understand the differences between employee styles and allow individuals to use their strengths to their fullest potential.

2. **Encourage continuing development.** The innate yearning to learn and grow is natural to human beings. Employees who are encouraged to expand their personal and professional development appreciate their jobs even more. A quality employer can set up a personal development library, even if this means the top of a credenza in the office.

Seminars and ongoing certification programs for your employees feed their personal development appetite. Many corporations hire personal coaches for their employees. Personal coaches work with employees on an individual basis to continue to give them the edge. These ongoing training ideas nurture your employees and expand their employable talents.

3. **Extend recognition and praise.** These are essential building blocks for employee retention. There is nothing complicated about recognition, but it continues to be one of the highest needs on employee's lists. Recognition can be received by way of verbal praise, with awards presentations, implementing an employee's suggestion (and giving them credit for it), and many other ways. The point is to extend praise regularly. Employees say they need a genuine pat on the back at least once a week. What a concept.

4. **Genuinely care about your employees.**
   Here is another bit of nuclear physics knowledge. Employees say this is at the top of
   their list for job satisfaction. When someone
   at work, either the employer or the manager,
   sincerely cares about them as a person, they
   tend to stay longer and have a much higher
   level of productivity. Employees that are
   treated as individuals and whose personal
   talents are respected are much more content
   to stay with your company.

5. **Salary and benefits are not the number
   one reason that people stay at a company.**
   Surprised? The fact is, according to one recent poll, employees say it is actually fifth on
   their list of top ten reasons to stay at a company. Other factors seem much more important. Work environment, people issues, and
   growth opportunities rate much higher than
   money and benefits. A good compensation

package is necessary in combination with these other factors.

6. **Offer regular, quality feedback.** A great manager or employer must have an understanding of the talents each employee possesses. Regular performance evaluations help the employee stay focused on their productivity. Objective feedback helps the employee continue to understand his role. Emphasis should be placed on their strengths and how best to use them. This will help the employee gain self-understanding and knowledge about the talents they possess and how they are applied every day at work.

7. **Nurture friendships at the office.** Human beings are very social by nature. Work is a place where long-term friendships are often developed. This evolution of quality relationships between people is very normal and it is a part of a healthy workplace. Employers understand that loyalties between their per-

sonnel can foster company loyalty. Set up an environment in which friendships can be developed and are able to grow. Company functions and team projects are a good way to make this happen.

8. **Provide the right tools.** Having the right resources and equipment for your people is essential. This allows them to do the best job with the latest tools. Simple things like adequate lighting, ergonomic furniture, product information guides, and computers that are networked together allow your people to do their job right.

9. **Include employees in the decision making process.** Great employers consult with employees regularly to make sure their ideas and instincts are recognized. Especially when decisions are made that affect an employee's position, it is most important to make them a part of the process. In doing this, you acknowledge the intelligence and

value of the employee. When their opinions count and credit is given to them for good ideas, they tend to stay in your employ.

10. **Allow them to make a difference.** When your team feels a sense of mission and purpose, their job has meaning and significance. They want to know they are contributing to an important endeavor. The best workplaces give their employees a sense of purpose, help them feel they belong, and enable them to make a difference.

## *Motivating Your Trade Contractors*

Finding good trade contractors, keeping good trade contractors, and having trade contractors represent your company in a professional manner is an ongoing challenge.

Like your employee associates, your trade contractors need you to take specific action to keep them motivated to make money for you.

Similarly, the first order of business is to drop the "sub-contractor" language from your vocabulary. Though it is very common, you must elevate your terminology in order to empower your tradespeople. From now on, refer to them as trade contractors, craftsmen or craftswomen, technicians, partners or associates. With this small shift in verbiage you will get their attention and gain their respect.

Here are ten extremely important strategies for motivating your trade contractors to make more money for you and to help them take more pride in their work.

1. **Be detail oriented.** Give them details about more than just the specifications of the project. Your trade contractors want details about every aspect of the project. Let them know about debris removal, parking location, safety procedures, emergency contact information, material storage, toilet facilities, payment method and schedule,

material list responsibility, smoking policy, music volume, and job access. Leave nothing to chance or to assumption.

2. **Communicate openly and regularly.** Your trade contractors need to know that they have an outlet for expressing any concerns they may have about your projects. They need to know who they can talk to and that they will be heard. They need to know exactly how their bid fits into the job budget and when they are expected to perform their services. Frequently discuss quality of work issues, project management issues, payment and pricing suggestions, customer satisfaction issues, safety concerns, and labor and time management. Keep the lines of communication open and candid.

3. **Give regular praise.** As with your employee associates, trade contractors need regular, specific recognition. The fact that they are independent business people does

not negate your responsibility to give praise where deserved. Trade contractors are real people too. They have feelings and concerns. Always praise them in public and offer criticism in private. If you want your trade contractors to really be motivated to perform, praise them aloud in front of your customers.

4. **Give them perks.** Give your trade contractors extras, e.g., hats, pencils, small tools, and T-shirts. If they finish a project ahead of schedule or under budget, give them tickets to a ball game or send their family to dinner at the local steak house. Bring donuts and coffee to the job once in a while for your trade contractor and their employees. While you probably want to minimize their interaction with your customers, they will inevitably build rapport with your clients and they can suggest changes in the project that may result in extra work orders

and more profit. You can offer a percentage or a commission when they bring in additional work. Since they are independent business owners, send them a lead every once in a while so that they can keep work in their business pipeline.

5. **Enthusiasm breeds enthusiasm.** In order for your trade contractors to be motivated and enthusiastic about your projects, you must take the lead. Your enthusiastic approach to your projects will influence your trade contractors to be the same way. Your opinions of your customers, your projects and the potential outcome of your projects are transferable to your trade contractors. They need your consistent positive attitude to help them understand the bigger picture of the projects they perform for you. They also need motivation to help them grow their business and to continue to improve their craft.

6. **Make them a part of your team.** Your trade contractors need to know that they are not alone. Everyone needs a community to be a part of. It is your job to convince your trade contractors that they are part of your team. Team members watch out for other team members. They all pull together to accomplish a specific job. Help them to understand that the actions of all team members impact other team members. Team players will accomplish more than individuals.

7. **Give regular, productive feedback.** They need constructive feedback about their quality of work and their customer service. Schedule and hold regular meetings with your craftspeople. Be specific and be helpful with them. Try this feedback formula. Give four or five specific points of praise. Give one or two points of feedback. Ask, "What would you suggest as a solution to

this challenge?" Listen intently and make them a partner in the solution. Ask for their feedback and suggestions about your company. Remember that this is a partnership and you also want to improve.

8. **Be loyal.** They need to know that you are loyal to them in front of your customer and that you will not overtly put the blame on them for problems on the job. They need to know that you awarded the project to them because of their skill and professionalism. They need to know that in the event of a budget difference, you will give them the first right of refusal and that you will come right back to them on the next project. Your trade contractors also need to know that you trust their judgement on the job when you are not there. Most importantly, they need to understand that you will continue to give them work as long as they perform.

9. **Provide disciplined systems.** Your trade contractors want to know that there is a specific systematic way that you run your business. They do not want you to be indecisive or coy with them. Give them a regular pattern of doing business that they can count on. This includes payment schedules, invoicing procedures, material list responsibilities, communication processes, warranty responsibilities, and more. When you display a steady dependable way of conducting business, your trade contractors will respond in kind.

10. **Give them business counseling.** Share your expertise and experience with your trade contractors. Help them to grow their business. Share your professional resources with them. Introduce them to your banker, your accountant, your broker and your insurance provider. Counsel them on systems, communications and employee

morale. When you help them strengthen their business, it will benefit you immensely.

Make a commitment to build a team of high quality employee associates and expert trades people. When your team is happy, they are much more productive. They represent you in a more professional manner and they help you to increase your profit power.

# CHAPTER TEN:

# UNLEASH THE LEADER IN YOU

## *Make an impact and leave a legacy*

Why are you in business? What is your motivation for doing what you do? Why do you show up each Monday morning to face another week of demanding customers, irritating trade contractors, impatient vendors, and unmotivated employees?

For many contractors in this country, the above description is all too vivid. I truly hope that it is not a reality in your business. However, the question still remains, "Why do you do what you do?"

When I first started educating contractors in 1999, the primary issue facing them was employee and trade contractor retention. The housing industry was the backbone of a booming national economy. As a result, contractors all around the country were busier than they had ever been. They were experiencing higher than normal employee and trade contractor turnover. It seems that the labor force was willing to move down the block for fifty cents more per square foot. Employees would change companies like you change socks. I taught solutions to those challenges and everyone seemed to get past the fury of the housing boom.

Over the last year, there has been a drastic change in what is most important to contractors. The economy has leveled out somewhat and the labor force is less transient.

Each year I speak at dozens of national conferences and construction industry conventions around the country. I am frequently asked to share my insights on the latest, hottest topic in the industry, leadership. Planning and preparing for the future, designing a compelling purpose for your enterprise, and leaving a legacy are at the top of the mental consciousness of highly successful construction entrepreneurs.

It all goes back to the original question presented at the outset of this chapter. Why do you do what you do? You may think of it in other, more familiar terms. What is the ultimate purpose for your enterprise? What legacy do you wish to create with your business? How do you develop future leaders for your business? Will you be able to leave your business in good hands when you decide to move to another phase of your life?

The answer to all of these questions whittles down to leadership. Your ability to lead your team effectively will determine what legacy you will leave. Your leadership abilities will determine your level of personal satisfaction in your business. What you create, who you inspire, and how you lead your company will be remembered long after you decide to transition to the next phase of your life.

What is leadership? Very simply, leadership is influence. It is your ability to affect the outcome of your business and to inspire others to act in your behalf. Leadership influence is demonstrated in two primary areas, people influence and personal influence.

People influence is your ability to motivate, inspire, and spark others to take action. People follow leaders because they sense a feeling of hope and optimism. Your trade contractors, employee associates, vendors, and peers will follow your lead based on your ability to enthusiastically convey your purposeful ideas to them.

The second primary area of leadership is your ability to demonstrate personal influence. In other words, your dedication to personal improvement will impact your leadership ability. Are you devoted to being the best you can be? Do you consistently search for ways to improve your health, your communication, your mind, your spirit and your emotional strength?

A leader takes people where they are unwilling to go on their own. Influential leaders have specific characteristics that they exhibit on a regular basis. Here are eight common traits that dynamic leaders possess. Grade yourself to see how you measure up to these traits.

1. **Humility.** Dynamic leaders are not arrogant. They do not seek their own advantage. They are concerned with serving the needs of their team. Leaders do not view their people as subordinates. They see everyone in their circle as fellow team members working toward the same goals. They do not presume that others will follow them as a result of their title or position. Dynamic leaders operate with a spirit of collaboration.

2. **Discipline.** Powerful leaders are disciplined and systematic about their planning process. They implement systems, policies and procedures that are easy to follow. They invest an appropriate amount of time to schedule their

activities. Dynamic leaders are driven toward excellence in everything they do.

3. **Risk taker.** Charismatic leaders take calculated risks. They are not necessarily gamblers by definition. By virtue of their discipline and planning, they know when to act in a situation. Dynamic leaders make quick decisions based on solid information and they stick to their decisions, rarely changing their mind for the sake of personal convenience.

4. **People savvy.** This trait is the single most important. Dynamic leaders know people. They understand what makes people react and what motivates people to take action. Powerful leaders communicate well with others. They understand that each person has a unique set of qualities and leaders have the innate capacity to match the right person with the right job. A leader gives you hope and inspiration when you are in their presence.

5. **Purpose driven.** Dynamic leaders understand the bigger picture of their enterprise. They work for more than just money. They see a greater purpose in everything they do. The acquisition of money and material possessions is rarely at the top of their list. Powerful leaders want to make a difference in the world and with other people.

6. **Vision oriented.** Dynamic leaders are very clear about what they want to accomplish. They have thought about it extensively. They have visualized their success and they see far beyond the present moment when they make decisions. They continually ask themselves the question, "How will my decisions impact the future of my company?"

7. **Perpetually positive.** Influential leaders see the glass as always full. The glass is full of something and dynamic leaders will find what it is. They have personal pride, integrity, and a glowing demeanor and are never flustered

by the potential of what could go wrong. Dynamic leaders are enthusiastic and they frequently seem "larger than life."

8. **Uncanny willingness to learn.** School is never out for dynamic leaders. They are constantly in search of better ways to do business and improve their professional existence. Powerful leaders are usually voracious readers and avoid watching too much television. They tend to share their wealth of knowledge with others as a way of enhancing what they have learned.

It is my belief that leaders are not born with these characteristics. They are developed. I believe that early life experiences may have influenced their way of thinking. However, they have learned their leadership skills through trial and experience. Leadership can be taught at an intellectual level, but those who plan to lead must develop their wisdom with real life situations.

# *Developing leaders in your organization*

If you are developing leaders in your organization, there are specific strategies that you can employ to enhance your leadership abilities. You must guide your future leaders in a way that will encourage them to make decisions for themselves.

Your team needs you to be actively involved in the transition of leadership in the following ways.

1. **Get down and dirty with them.** An effective leader never asks the team to do something that they would not do themselves. Show up on the job site and get construction dust all over you. Feel free to crawl on your knees with your people and show them that you will do whatever it takes to make your project a success.

2. **Communicate clearly and be candid.** Future leaders need to have toughness in their skin. You should be able to speak candidly to them about your expectations. Share with them your vision and tell them exactly what you expect from them as future leaders. If they are offended or overly sensitive, they may need more time to develop.

3. **Set ethical standards and be an example.** If you expect your future leaders to operate from a set of high moral and ethical values, then lead by example. There should not be a hint of impropriety in your operation. Show them how to settle disagreements in a professional, first class manner. Teach them to treat everyone fairly and with respect.

4. **Invest in their education.** Send your future leaders to seminars, certification programs, and professional development workshops. Share your audio programs, books, videos, and educational materials with them. Have

frequent mind-storming sessions and teach them the nuances of your business. Help them to understand why things work the way they do.

5. **Prioritize for them and with them.** Organizational skills are sorely lacking in many segments of American society. Educate your future leaders to plan, prepare, prioritize, systematize, and work on the most important things first. Tutor them to identify what will earn the most profits in the most efficient manner. Help them to understand that change is inevitable and that they must adapt to new situations while keeping in mind their priorities.

6. **Emphasize people over production.** Mentor your future leaders to understand that without motivated people, they are nothing. Teach them to develop their people as you have developed them. Help them to understand the value of every human. When you

train them to be people minded, production will inevitably take care of itself.

**7. Give affirmation and encouragement.** Even though you may be working with highly motivated, self-starting future leaders, they still need your encouragement. Give them your regular praise and reassurance. Help them to see that they will make great leaders themselves. Encourage them to stretch beyond their comfort zones to develop their own leadership style. Offer your genuine support and be their greatest advocate.

## Leave a legacy

Do you have a compelling purpose for your business? The ultimate reason for your entrepreneurial endeavor must be more than money or material gain. It must be more than just trying to make a living. The existence of your business should encompass the grander scheme of things. There are any number of compelling reasons you could have. Here are just a few for you to consider.

- Contribution to your community

- A genuine expression of your creativity and individuality

- Developing a viable business for future generations of your heirs

- Testimony of your personal faith in your heavenly creator

- Declaration of your commitment to honor the gift of life itself

- Leaving a legacy of excellence, dedication and devotion

- Display of your ethical values and personal integrity

- Raising the level of professionalism in the industry

You may think of other compelling reasons to operate your construction enterprise. Your ability to unleash the powerful leader in you will be enhanced when you identify a driving force that is both noble and just.

The construction industry needs powerful leaders now more than ever. The industry is rapidly changing. Technological advances are making the business more competitive and more available to new entrepreneurs. Make leadership a commitment for life. Create a culture of leadership. Nurture potential leaders and leave your mark, your legacy on this industry.

# THE FINAL PUNCH LIST

In order to increase your profit power you must have a commitment to excellence. Profits do not just happen. Profits do not necessarily increase because you have the best customer service or the best product in town. Increased profits are not guaranteed because you have a fancy marketing scheme or a great reputation.

Increasing the profit power of your business begins with your dedication to long-term success. It is a combination of events, planning and a lot of persistence and sweat equity.

The ten strategies that I have presented in this book are the foundation for your construction business success. Here is a very quick overview, the final punch list of these strategies and what they will do for you.

1. **Be a Sales Magnet**. Create irresistibility by connecting with your customers, pros-

pects and team members at a deep meaningful level. Be genuine and seek agreement with others. You will attract more sales and increase your profit power.

2. **Get Top Dollar**. In order to establish the real value of your operation you must find out from your premier customer what they really want. Be responsible, knowledgeable, and dedicated to quality. You will set yourself apart in an intensely competitive marketplace to increase your profit power.

3. **The Contractor's Private Entrance Door**. Create partnerships with your customers. It is a matter of attitude, establishing mutual goals and seeing complaints and challenges as an opportunity to get better. Customer partnerships will reduce problems and increase your profit power.

4. **Develop Your Personal Excellence**. Transform your life and your business by committing to excellent communication skills and investing in your personal growth. There is a direct connection between personal growth and increased profit power.

5. **Thinking Outside the Sale**. Lighten up. Enjoy the selling process. Be natural and be yourself. Think of unique ways to express your value and the value of your product. Do something different from your competitors and you will increase your profit power.

6. **Why Hurry Up and Wait?** Make the bidding process work for you by investing $3.49 in a "DRAFT COPY" rubber stamp. Working with your prospects and staying in constant communication with them while you are bidding their project will result in increasing your profit power.

7. **How to Maximize Your Publicity**. A top 10 list of low-cost publicity strategies will help you to have a fresh marketing approach. These strategies will definitely help you increase your profit power.

8. **"All Systems Go"**. Create standard operating procedures for your company. Have your policies and procedures well documented. Your people will operate your systems. Your systems will operate your business and that will increase your profit power.

9. **Teaming up for Success.** Motivate your trade contractors and employee associates to be more productive. Create an environment of trust and respect with your team. Happy team members translate to increased profit power.

10. **Unleash the Leader in You.** Posses the eight common traits of dynamic lead-

ers. Develop future leaders in your organization. Create a compelling vision and purpose for your enterprise and this will lead to increasing your long-term profit power.

I would be remiss if I didn't take my own advice. In chapter seven, I made the point that you must ask for what you want. If you want more business, ask for it. If you want more leads, more referrals, more publicity, more sales, more profits, ask for them.

I am going to lead by example. I won't ask you for anything impossible. I just want a few things that will help me continue the work I do with contractors.

Very simply, I am asking for three things.

First, send me your feedback on the strategies in this book. I want to know what works for you and what needs to work better. I want to know what else you need to increase your business and your profit power. If you have a personal success story as a result of this book, send it to me via email. When you do, I will reward you with five free books for your friends and colleagues. Send your feedback and comments to **Paul@ContractorOfChoice.com.**

Second, register on-line for my free electronic newsletter.

Log on to **www.ContractorOfChoice.com** and sign up for my monthly electronic newsletter. Tell five of your closest friends and colleagues to do the same.

Third and finally, do something good for our industry. Contribute your time, your energy, your money, and your expertise to a good cause in your local community. If you want the recognition for your contribution, that is fine. If you just want to do it because it is the right thing to do, congratulations. There are those in our so-

ciety less fortunate than you. Please do something to help support them.

# ABOUT THE AUTHOR

### *(Shameless promotion time)*

Paul Montelongo is a nationally recognized speaker, author, and consultant to the construction industry and related industries. Paul speaks regularly at national conventions and for private corporate events.

He is the author of *101 Power Strategies; Tools to Promote Yourself as the Contractor of Choice.* This 144-page guide to marketing and promotional concepts has been wildly successful in the construction industry. It is currently in its third printing and plans are in place for its fourth edition.

Paul conducts leadership workshops, sales and marketing seminars and project management programs for professional contractors all around North America. He is an approved trainer for the Home Builders Institute. HBI is the education and training arm of the National Association of Home Builders.

Paul earned the prestigious Certified Graduate Remodelor™ designation from the National Association of Home Builders in 2002. The CGR designation recognizes excellence and professional commitment to the construction industry in America.

As if that weren't enough, Paul has also formed an alliance with ProNetworks TV to create two Internet based educational TV channels specifically for contractors.

**www.BuilderChannel.TV** is the educational channel designed for custom and production home builders and their vendor partners.

**www.RemodelerChannel.TV** is the educational channel designed for professional remodeling contractors and their vendor partners.

Please log in to the channel of your profession and preview the programs that will help you most in your business.

Paul lives in San Antonio, Texas (home of the 2003 World Champion San Antonio Spurs) with his wife and two sons.

If you would like more information about training, personal coaching, or seminar facilitation for your organization, call Paul toll free at 866-494-1911. Or you may send an email to **Paul@ContractorOfChoice.com**.

# An Open Invitation to My Contractor Peers and Colleagues

*"I feel like my business is running my life instead of me running my business. Between customers, sub-contractors and employees, I just can't seem to get ahead."*

Does that sound like your situation? I hope not, however if it does, you are not alone. That is the sentiment of many contractors who attend my seminars and workshops. The construction industry is a demanding profession. Customers cannot wait to get their project finished. Sub-contractors show up when they want to, and employees just seem to be working only to pull a check on Friday afternoon.

Then, there is highly competitive pricing and it seems like a new company pops up every six months to challenge your place in the market. It can create a viscous cycle with no apparent end in sight. What is the answer?

## *I will get to that in a minute.*

But first, let me tell you that when I decided a few years ago that I wanted to run a marathon, I knew that if I were going to reach my goal, I would need help. I would need someone with some real life running experience to keep me on track. As it turned out, I ended up with two coaches. One of them holds the record for running 1000 miles in 11 days and the other had run 38 marathons. The result: I have run four full 26.2 mile marathons and eight 13.1 mile half-marathons.

With those kinds of results, I began to look for coaches for other areas of my life. I have found them and they help me keep my life on track to accomplish the goals I have set.

Something else occurred. I had to have a radical shift in my mind set. You see, since the age of thirteen I wanted to run a marathon. But that little voice way down deep inside would say, "Who do you think you are Paul? You can't run a marathon. You haven't got what it takes."...and for twenty-five years, that voice was right, until...

I learned to change my thinking and my consciousness about what was possible. Therein lies the key to your success. When you are able to change your thinking, when you are able to shed limiting beliefs about what you can do and when you are able to get in touch with your inner strength and consciousness, then the possibilities are endless.

It takes a genuine awareness of what is working and what needs to get better. I have heard it said that the definition of insanity is doing the same things over and over and getting the same poor result.

*If you want to change your life, change your thinking and your expectations of yourself.*

But you may say, "Hey Montelongo, I am already successful. I have a great business and a great life."

I understand completely, because I said that, too, for many years. And by all the common societal standards, it is true. I live in a 3,500 sq.ft custom built home, take nice vacations, drive new cars, have a thriving business, am in great physical condition and have a wonderful family.

But that isn't enough. A sense of inner peace of mind and soul along with life balance is much more important.

And here is the most revealing thing about having a life of balance. When your level of consciousness rises, so does your prosperity. I am talking about all areas of prosperity. What you can create and give back to your community, your family, your peers and yourself far out-weighs any so-called material wealth.

## *And that is why I am writing to you.*

Sometimes it takes a different set of eyes and ears to get us on the right track. Sometimes it takes someone who has "been there and done that" to point out the tremendous power that is within you. And that is what coaching is all about.

What is coaching? How does it work? What benefits will you gain? This program is not for everyone, but if you are committed to flourishing in the marathon of your business and personal life, then this program may be for you.

With 26 years of experience as the owner and creator of two multi-million dollar construc-tion companies, i have "been in the trenches." I invite you to take a serious look my contractor coaching program and if you are interested in knowing more, please contact me by email at **Paul@ContractorOfChoice.com** or toll free at **866.494.1911** for a free initial coaching conversation.

There is great potential in each and every one of you to create the life you desire. Coaching is a premier way to help you unleash the unlimited power within you.

I hope that you give serious consideration to having a career coach. Obviously spaces are limited. I would hate for you to miss out on this extraordinary opportunity! Think about what this type of program could mean to you.

May you prosper and have great inner peace.

Paul Montelongo

# CONTRACTOR COACHING TERMS AND CONDITIONS

The following terms and conditions are intended to explain most of the common questions about the Contractor Coaching Program. If you have any additional questions, send an email to **Paul@ContractorOfChoice.com** or call me toll free at **866.494.1911**.

1. First and most important, I want you to be successful. I want this process to result in your personal and professional success. You are the determining factor in your success and you will get the most from your investment if you do the work and put into practice the coaching. I will only be your coach. You are the player in the game. I will compliment you. I will challenge you. I will encourage you and I will certainly push you, but the final results are up to you.

2. What is Contractor Coaching? It is a way for an experienced, seasoned construction industry pro-

fessional (me) to be matched up with a construction industry entrepreneur (you) on a regular bimonthly basis. This match is intended to get you to take a long hard look at what is happening in your business and life to make things work better. The coaching arrangement is intended to get you to "close the gap". You will determine precisely where you are today and where you want to be in the future. A Coach is the unbiased third party that helps you bridge the gap. A Coach is more than a mentor is and much more than a consultant. A Coach works with you to give personal attention and direction with your life and business. The greatest athletes and business entrepreneurs in the world have coaches. Tiger Woods has a coach. Fortune 500 executives have coaches. I have coaches and you should too.

3. There is no charge for a half-hour pre-coaching interview and initial coaching session. Try it to see how the format works for you and what benefits you will derive from an ongoing coaching session.

4. Your time is valuable and so is mine. My schedule only allows me room for about 10 coaching clients at any one time. I will interview you to see if our time together can be productive. After the interview, we can set up the specific time for your bi-monthly call. If I am booked up with coaching clients or feel like someone else will better serve you, I will let you know that.

5. Your monthly investment includes the following:

    a) Two to six half-hour telephone calls each month set at a specific time each week.

    b) Four email correspondences for questions and answers to your personal or professional issues or just to check in to measure your progress. (I suggest you use these once a week for spaced repetition)

    c) A complete review of all of your printed or electronic marketing materials, contracts, brochures, sales letters, internal office forms and proposal forms.

d) My assessment of those materials with a complete feedback analysis of your materials. This will be done twice; once at the beginning of your coaching program and once six months later.

e) One copy of each of my books: 101 Power Strategies; Tools to Promote Yourself as the Contractor of Choice and one copy of Profit Power; Ten Strategies to Blueprint a Dynamic Construction Business.

f) You may attend any of the classes in my Tele-seminar series free of charge.

6. You may "opt-out" of the monthly coaching arrangement anytime with 30 days notice. No harm, no hard feelings and no further obligation. I wish you the very best.

7. After the first year of coaching we will do an in-depth analysis of your success and your goals for the future. At that time, we will assess the possibilities for the next 12 months. You should know that most of my coaching arrangements last six to

nine months. That usually is plenty of time to make the proper adjustments.

8. The monthly investment ranges from $350 to $500 per month. It depends on the number of phone calls that we agree to. You may invest in additional coaching or consulting with me at any-time. I will discuss fees with you at that time.

9. You may pay with your Visa, Master Card, Discover, American Express or check. Your Coaching investment fee will be charged on your credit card the first of each month.

10. If you pay by check, your check must be received in our office prior to your first official Coaching call. Checks are made payable to Paul Montelongo Enterprises, Inc. and mailed to 1141 N Loop 1604 East, Suite 105, PMB 407, San Antonio, Texas 78232.

11. Know this: I have built a very solid contracting career and sold tens of millions of dollars of projects by delivering more to my customers than I ever promised. And many times, I promised

pretty big. It is in my nature to do that. My wife says that I could run 2 or 3 miles a few times a week and stay in great shape. She wonders why I choose to run 26.2-mile marathons instead. I figure you are only on this planet a short while, so if you are going to be in the game, you may as well play all out.

I am looking forward to a great coaching experience with you.

Take great care.

Paul Montelongo

# SUGGESTED READING

There have been many books that have influenced my professional and personal life. Here is a short list of the books I have personally studied and recommend to you.

Ailes, Roger. 1988. *You Are the Message.* New York: Doubleday.

Albrecht, Karl. 1994. *The Northbound Train.* New York: Amacom

Andreas, Steve and Connie. 1987. *Change Your Mind and Keep the Change.* Moab, UT: Real People Press.

Bandler, Richard and Grindler, John. 1979. *Frogs into Princes, Neuro Linguistic Programming.* Moab, UT: Real People Press

Beckwith, Harry, 1997. *Selling the Invisible.* New York: Warner Books.

Belasco, James A. and Stayer, Ralph C. 1993. *Flight of the Buffalo: Soaring to Excellence, Learning to Let Employees Lead.* New York: Warner Books.

Blanchard, Kenneth. 1985. *The One Minute Manager.* New York: Berkeley Publishing.

Blanchard, Kenneth and Peale, Norman Vincent. 1988. *The Power of Ethical Management.* New York: William Morrow and Company.

Blanchard, Kenneth and Oncken, William and Burrows, Hal. 1989. *The One Minute Manager Meets the Monkey.* New York: William Morrow and Company.

Brooks, William T. 1988. *High Impact Selling; Power Strategies for Successful Selling.* Gameplan Press

Brown, Les. 1997. *It's Not Over Until You Win.* New York: Fireside Books.

Buckingham, Marcus and Coffman, Curt. *First, Break All The Rules: What the World's Greatest Managers Do Differently.*

Canfield, Jack and Hansen, Mark Victor. 2000 *The Power of Focus.* Health Communications, Inc.

Carlson, Richard Dr. 1997. *Don't Sweat the Small Stuff.* New York: Hyperion.

Carnegie, Dale. 1936. *How To Win Friends and Influence People.* New York: Simon & Schuster.

Cialdini, Robert, B. PhD. 1984. *Influence. The Psychology of Persuasion.* New York: William Morrow Company.

Cousins, Norman. 1979. *The Anatomy of an Illness As Perceived by The Patient.* New York: W.W. Norton & Company.

Covey, Stephen R. 1990. *Principle-Centered Leadership.* New York: Summit Books.

Covey, Stephen R. 1989. *The 7 Habits of Highly Effective People.* New York: Simon and Schuster.

Daley, Kevin 1996. *Socratic Selling, How to Ask Questions that Get the Sale.* McGraw-Hill.

Dyer, Wayne Dr. 1989. *You'll See It When You Believe It.* New York: Avon Books.

Heath, Jinger. 1998. *Positively You. Change Your Thinking, Change Your Life.* New York: Golden Books.

Hill, Napoleon. 1937. *Think and Grow Rich.* New York: Plume Books

Hopkins, Tom. 1983. *How to Master the Art of Selling.* New York: Warner Books.

Knight, Sue. 1995. *NLP at Work. The difference That Makes a Difference in Business.* London: Nicholas Brealey Publishing.

Karmer, Marc. 1998. *Power Networking.* Chicago:NTC/Contemporary Publishing Company.

Leonard, Thomas J. 1998. *The Portable Coach.* New York: Scribner Publishing.

Mackay, Harvey. 1998. *Dig Your Well Before You're Thirsty.* New York: Doubleday.

MacKenzie, Gordon. 1996. *Orbiting the Giant Hairball.* New York: Viking Press.

McCormack, Mark H. 1984. *What They Don't Teach You at Harvard Business School.* New York: Bantam Books.

Montelongo, Paul. 2001. *101 Power Strategies; Tools to Promote Yourself as The Contractor of Choice.* Sioux Falls, SD Pinehill Press

Montelongo, Paul. 2003. *Profit Power; Ten Strategies to Blueprint a Dynamic Construction Business.* San Antonio, TX Success Concepts, Inc.

Pitino, Rick. 1997. *Success is a Choice.* New York: Broadway Books.

Richardson, Jerry. 1987. *The Magic of Rapport.* Capitola, CA: Meta Publications.

Roane, Susan. 1993. *The Secrets of Savvy Networking.* New York: Warner Books.

Robbins, Anthony. 1991. *Awaken the Giant Within.* New York: Fireside Books.

Strunk, William and White, E.B. 1979. *The Elements of Style.* Boston: Allyn and Bacon.

Von Oech, Roger Dr. 1983. *A Whack on the Side of the Head.* Menlo Park, CA: Creative Think.

# ORDER FORM

Yes, I want more copies of this fantastic book to give to my friends, colleagues, employees, trade contractors, banker, accountant, and anyone else I may think of.

Profit Power; Ten Strategies to Blueprint a Dynamic Construction Business

_____ copies @ $20.00 each =_____
+$3.50 each S&H= $_____

Make Check Payable to Paul Montelongo Enterprises, Inc.

☐ Check here if you wish to receive information about workshops, consulting, or keynote presentations by Paul Montelongo for your business or professional association.

☐ Check here if you wish to receive Paul's free electronic newsletter. Receive tips, strategies, and coaching to promote yourself as the Contractor of Choice and create more Profit Power.

Your email address is:

_____.

■     Mail or fax to:

Paul Montelongo Enterprises, Inc.
1141 N. Loop 1604 East
Suite 105, PMB 407
San Antonio, Texas 78232
Fax: 210.494.3882

Name: _____

Company: _____

Position: _____

City, State, Zip: _____

E-mail: _____

Credit Card #: _____

Expiration Date: _____

Signature: _____

Visit **www.PaulMontelongo.com** or
**www.ContractorOfChoice.com**
Or call toll free **866.494.1911**.